SCIENTIFIC AMERICAN EDUCATIONAL PUBLISHING

COOKING WITH CHEMISTRY

10 FUN FOOD SCIENCE PROJECTS

BRING SCIENCE HOME

Published in 2025 by Scientific American Educational Publishing in association with The Rosen Publishing Group.

Contains material from Scientific American, a division of Springer Nature America, Inc., reprinted by permission as well as original material from The Rosen Publishing Group.

First Edition

Editor: Kristen Rajczak Nelson
Designer: Rachel Rising

Activity on page 5 by Science Buddies (January 26, 2012); page 11 by Science Buddies, Sabine De Brabandere (January 10, 2019); page 19 by Science Buddies, Megan Arnett (August 16, 2018); page 23 by Science Buddies, Megan Arnett (July 27, 2017); page 27 by Science Buddies, Sabine De Brabandere (September 19, 2019); page 33 by Science Buddies, Svenja Lohner (April 11, 2019); page 39 by Science Buddies, Megan Arnett (September 13, 2018); page 43 by Science Buddies (September 1, 2016); page 49 by Science Buddies, Megan Arnett (June 21, 2018); page 55 by Science Buddies (March 28, 2013).

All illustrations by Continuum Content Solutions

Photo Credits: pp. 4, 5, 11, 19, 23, 27, 33, 39, 43, 49, 55 Anna Frajtova/Shutterstock.com; pp. 3, 4, 5, 8, 11, 15, 27, 31, 33, 36, 43, 46, 47, 55, 58 Anna Frajtova/Shutterstock.com.

Library of Congress Cataloging-in-Publication Data

Names: Scientific American, inc., editor.
Title: Cooking with chemistry : 10 fun food science projects / Scientific American, editors.
Description: Buffalo, NY : Scientific American Educational Publishing, an imprint of Rosen Publishing, [2025] | Series: Bring science home | Includes bibliographical references and index.
Identifiers: LCCN 2023054902 (print) | LCCN 2023054903 (ebook) | ISBN 9781725350526 (library binding) | ISBN 9781725350519 (paperback) | ISBN 9781725350533 (ebook)
Subjects: LCSH: Food--Experiments--Juvenile literature. | Science--Experiments--Juvenile literature. | Cooking--Experiments--Juvenile literature.
Classification: LCC TX355 .C7155 2025 (print) | LCC TX355 (ebook) | DDC 641.30078--dc23/eng/20231221
LC record available at https://lccn.loc.gov/2023054902
LC ebook record available at https://lccn.loc.gov/2023054903

Manufactured in the United States of America

CPSIA Compliance Information: Batch #CSSA25. For further information contact Rosen Publishing, New York, New York at 1-800-237-9932.

CONTENTS

THESE ACTIVITIES INCLUDE SCIENCE FAIR PROJECT IDEAS.

INTRODUCTION

Cooking may be a job that your parents normally do, but there are fun and interesting ways that you can help to cook . . . with science! Explore different techniques to boil an egg, experiments that teach about acids and bases, and tasty ideas to make your own slushies, lemonade, and boba in these engaging and interesting activities.

Projects marked with include a section called Science Fair Project Ideas. These ideas can help you develop your own original science fair project. Science fair judges tend to reward creative thought and imagination, and it helps if you are really interested in your project. You will also need to follow the scientific method. See page 61 for more information about that.

Cabbage Chemistry
Finding Acids and Bases

EXPLORE ACIDS AND BASES USING CABBAGE IN THIS CHEMISTRY EXPERIMENT.

You might have done experiments with well-labeled acids and bases in school, but have you ever wondered whether a certain food or chemical around the house is an acid or a base? You can find out using a red cabbage to make an indicator solution.

When two or more ingredients are entirely dissolved in one another, you have a solution. For example, mixing salt with water creates a clear solution, even though the salt is there and the solution tastes salty. When mixed with water, whether a chemical "donates" a charged particle (called an ion) to the solution—in this case, a hydrogen ion—or "accepts" one from it determines whether it's an acidic or basic solution. An indicator changes color when exposed to such a mixture, depending on whether the solution is acidic or basic.

PROJECT TIME

1 hour

KEY CONCEPTS

Chemistry
Acids
Bases
Light

BACKGROUND

Acids are solutions that lose hydrogen ions and usually taste sour. Some very common household solutions are acids, such as citrus fruit juices and household vinegar. Bases are solutions that pull hydrogen ions out of solution and onto themselves, "accepting" them, and usually feel slippery. Bases have many practical uses. For example, "antacids" such as TUMS are used to reduce the acidity in your stomach. Other bases make useful household cleaning products.

To tell if something is an acid or a base, you can use a chemical called an indicator. An indicator changes color when it encounters an acid or base. There are many different types of indicators, some that are liquids and others that are concentrated on little strips of "litmus" paper. Indicators can be extracted from many different sources, including the pigment of many plants. For example, red cabbages contain an indicator pigment molecule called flavin, which is a type of molecule called an anthocyanin. Very acidic solutions will turn an anthocyanin red whereas neutral solutions will make it purplish, and basic solutions will turn it greenish-yellow. Consequently, the color an anthocyanin solution turns can be used to determine a solution's pH—a measure of how basic or acidic a solution is.

MATERIALS

- A small red cabbage
- Pot of boiling water
- Strainer
- Two large bowls or pots
- Grater
- Tablespoon measuring spoon
- Large spoon (optional)
- Three or more small, white paper cups (small, white paper drinking glasses or dishes will also work)
- Goggles or other protective eyewear
- Lemon or lime juice
- Vinegar
- Bleach-based cleaning product
- Other foods to test, such as clear soda pop, baking soda solution, egg whites, tomatoes, cottage cheese (optional)

PREPARATION

- Grate a small red cabbage. If you do not want to grate the entire cabbage, grating half of a cabbage should be enough. Put the fine, pulpy grated cabbage into a large bowl or pot.
- Boil a pot of water. Use caution when handling the boiling water. Pour the boiling water into the bowl with the cabbage pulp until the water just covers the cabbage.
- Leave the cabbage mixture steeping, stirring occasionally, until the liquid is room temperature. This should take at least half an hour. The liquid will become red or purplish-red in color.
- Place a strainer over another large bowl or pot and pour the cabbage mixture through the strainer to remove the cabbage pulp. Press down on the pulp in the strainer, such as by using a large spoon, to squeeze more liquid out of the pulp.
- In the bowl, you should now have only liquid that will either be purple or blue in color. This will be your indicator solution, which you will use to test the pH of different liquids.
- You should wear goggles or other protective eyewear and adults should supervise and use caution when handling bleach and vinegar, because they can irritate eyes and skin.

PROCEDURE

- Fill a small, white paper cup, drinking glass or white dish with 1 tablespoon (15 ml) of your cabbage-indicator solution. *What is the color of your indicator solution?*
- Add drops of lemon or lime juice to the indicator solution until you see the solution change in color. Gently swirl the solution and make sure the color stays the same. *What color did the solution become?*
- The color of the solution will change depending on its pH: red color indicates the pH is 2; purple indicates pH 4; violet indicates pH 6; blue indicates pH 8; blue-green indicates pH 10; greenish-yellow indicates pH 12.

- *Based on its color, what is the pH of the lemon or lime juice solution?*
- In another small, white paper cup, add 1 tablespoon (15 ml) of your original cabbage-indicator solution. Add drops of vinegar until you see the solution change color. *What color did the vinegar solution become? What is the pH of the solution?*
- In a third small, white paper cup, add 1 tablespoon (15 ml) of your original cabbage-indicator solution. Handling it with caution, add drops of the bleach cleaning product until you see the solution change color. *What color did the bleach solution become, and what does this indicate about its pH?*
- If you want to test the pH of other foods, add 1 tablespoon (15 ml) of your original cabbage-indicator solution to a small, white paper cup and add drops of the food until you see the solution change color. If the food is not in liquid form, crush it or dissolve it in a small amount of water before adding it to the indicator solution. *What color did the solution become, and what does this indicate about its pH?*

SCIENCE FAIR IDEA

There are other vegetables and fruits that can be used to make pH indicators as well: red onion, apple skins, blueberries, grape skins, and plums. *Which different sources of pigment produce the best indicators?*

EXTRA

You can use an indicator solution to write secret messages. Just use full-strength lemon juice to write an invisible message on paper and let the message dry. To reveal the message, paint cabbage-indicator over the paper with a paintbrush.

OBSERVATIONS AND RESULTS

Did the indicator solution change color when you added the lime or lemon juice, vinegar, and bleach? Did the solution color indicate that the lime or lemon juice and vinegar were acidic (had a lower pH) and that the bleach was basic (with a higher pH)?

A solution with a pH between 5 and 7 is neutral, 8 or higher is a base, and 4 or lower is an acid. Lime juice, lemon juice, and vinegar are acids, so they should have turned the indicator solution red or purple color. Bleach is a strong base, therefore it should have turned the indicator solution a greenish-yellow color.

How basic or acidic a solution is depends on the amount of hydrogen ions in it. A basic solution accepts hydrogen ions (or donates electron pairs as hydroxide ions) whereas an acidic solution donates hydrogen ions (or accepts electron pairs). An indicator, like anthocyanin, responds to the levels of hydrogen ions in the solution. Anthocyanin and other biological pigments absorb certain wavelengths of light and reflect others, and it is the reflected light we see that makes them appear a certain color. Depending on the levels of hydrogen ions in the solution, the indicator pigment undergoes a chemical reaction that changes its chemical structure, making it reflect a different wavelength of light and thereby change color.

CLEANUP

Dilute the bleach solution with water before pouring it down a drain. (Remember to keep your goggles on when you do this.)

Chill Out by Making Homemade Slushies

LEARN HOW TO MAKE A FAVORITE FROZEN DRINK AT HOME USING A LITTLE KITCHEN CHEMISTRY.

Do you enjoy ice-cold drinks? A slushy is about as close as you can get to liquid ice: colder than water but more drinkable than ice! Using some common household items, a little bit of patience, and the help of science, you can make this delicious, sweet drink at home. Try this activity, and you will be rewarded with a delightful treat!

PROJECT TIME

30 minutes, plus at least 5 hours of freezing time

KEY CONCEPTS

Chemistry
Food science
Freezing
Solutions

BACKGROUND

A slushy is a dense, ice-cold beverage that resembles the thickness of melting snow. Slushies can be made in two ways: You can flavor finely crushed ice, or you can alter the freezing process of flavored water so that loose, icy crystals form. Shaking the liquid while keeping it at the freezing point does just that.

The freezing point of a substance is the temperature at which the substance changes from a liquid to a solid. For pure water (H_2O), this is 32°F (0°C). At this temperature, water particles start to stick together and form a lattice, or a crystalline hard structure.

Dissolving salt in pure water lowers its freezing point. This happens because the salt particles are in the way, making it harder for the water particles to stick together. This phenomenon is called freezing point depression. Salt is not the only substance that lowers water's freezing point, but it is a very effective one that is commonly available. Dissolving other particles such as sugar has a smaller but similar effect. In general, the more particles that are floating around in a fixed volume of water, the lower its freezing point will be.

Curious to know how freezing point depression can help us make slushies at home? Do this activity to find out!

MATERIALS

- Water
- Table salt
- Measuring cups
- Teaspoon
- Small mixing bowl
- Four zipper-lock sandwich bags
- Freezer
- Gloves or a towel
- Two smoothie shakers or 32-ounce food containers with lid, preferably translucent or transparent
- Fruit juice—for example, orange, apple, or grape juice (Do not use a sugar-free version.)
- Food coloring (optional)
- Thermometer that can go to -12°C or 10°F (optional)
- Soda or fruit-flavored syrup (optional)

PREPARATION

- Pour 1/2 cup (118 ml) of water into a bowl. Add 1 teaspoon of salt and stir until it is dissolved. If you have food coloring, you can mix in one or two drops. This will give your special ice a nice color—and makes it easier to detect leaked saltwater solution in your slushy.
- Pour the contents in a zipper-lock bag. Close the bag and set it aside.
- Repeat the previous two steps three more times until you have four zipper-lock bags of saltwater solution.
- Store the bags for at least five hours or overnight in the freezer. Make sure the bags do not touch one another so they do not freeze together.
- Store at least 1 cup (236 ml) of juice and 1 cup (236 ml) of water in the refrigerator.

PROCEDURE

- After five hours, check if the four saltwater solution bags in the freezer are frozen. If not, wait a few hours longer before proceeding.
- Take the frozen bags of saltwater solution from the freezer using gloves or a towel to protect your hands. For each bag, open the zipper, push the air from the bags and close the zipper again.
- Touch the bag with ice briefly with your fingers. If you have a thermometer, measure how cold this ice is. Regular ice cubes are 32°F (0°C). *Does this ice feel colder than regular ice cubes? Did the thermometer confirm what you felt? Why would you need this special ice to prepare a slushy?*
- Take the juice and water from the refrigerator. Pour 1 cup (236 ml) of juice in a shaker or food container. Rinse the measuring cup and pour 1 cup (236 ml) of water in the other shaker or food container.

- Put two of the sealed zipper-lock bags with frozen saltwater solution into each container before closing the lid.
- Shake one container a couple of times. Look through the sides of the container. Repeat with the other container. *How do the liquids drip down from the sides of the container?*
- Place your containers down and count slowly to 20 before repeating the previous step. Do this for several minutes. *Does the way the liquids drip from the sides of the containers change? Why would this happen? Does it happen at the same time in both containers?*
- Open the container after about three minutes. *Do you see hints of slush? Do you see a similar amount in both containers?*
- Close the containers and continue shaking intermittently.
- Once you see a thick mass sliding down the sides of a container, open the container again and look inside. *Do you have a slushy? How did the special ice in the bags change? Why would it have changed?*
- If the special bag of ice still has solid pieces of ice inside, you can close the container and continue shaking intermittently to make a denser slushy. *Why, however, might it not be a good idea to continue if the special ice has melted?*
- If the special ice has melted, take out the bags of salt water and set them aside. If salt water has leaked in your slushy, discard the slushy, freeze the zipper-lock bags with saltwater solution after rinsing them and try again.
- There is a possibility the juice never turned into a slushy. If your juice did not freeze, refreeze the zipper-lock bags with saltwater solution after rinsing the outside and dissolving an additional 1/2 teaspoon of salt in each. *Why do you think your juice did not turn into a slushy? Do you think you can solve this by adding more salt to the solution in the bags? Why or why not?*

- Pour the slushy content into a glass. If you have diluted syrup or soda, pour some over the slushy made with just water, mix well and drink. *Drink your juice slushy as is. Is one slushy better than the other?*

EXTRA

Find out if it is easier to first mix syrup in with the water and make a slushy of the mixture or to mix in the syrup after you have created slush from the water alone. *Why would this be the case? Which way tastes best?*

EXTRA

Try other juices. *Which juice is easiest to transform into a slushy?*

EXTRA

Can you find ways to make a larger slushy?

SCIENCE FAIR IDEA

Find out what happens if you mix more salt into the water to create the special ice. *What is the coldest special ice you can make?*

EXTRA

Test and see what happens if you do not shake the containers while making the slush.

OBSERVATIONS AND RESULTS

Did water turn into slush faster than juice did? Juice freezes at a lower temperature compared with water, so it needs to cool over a longer period before ice crystals appear.

Pure water freezes at 32°F (0°C). Adding particles to water makes it freeze at a lower temperature. That is why the salt water you made in this activity felt so cold when you took it out of the freezer. While making the slushy, it absorbed heat from the liquids in the containers. This process melted the saltwater ice as it cooled the liquids.

Fruit juice is made of fruit sugars dissolved in water together with some other particles, such as vitamins and minerals. Because fruit juice contains pure water with particles dissolved in it, it freezes at a lower temperature than pure water does. Most often its freezing point is not as low as that of the salt water you created, so the frozen salt water could still freeze the juice, although it did so more slowly than it could freeze water.

CLEANUP

If you would like to make more slushies later, you can reuse the zipper-lock bags with saltwater solution after rinsing and refreezing them. To discard them, you can dispose of them in the sink.

The Business of Fizziness

Find Your Soda's Fizz

HOW DOES YOUR SODA FIZZ? USE SOME SCIENCE TO FIND OUT ABOUT GASES HIDING IN SODA—AND HOW YOU CAN MAKE THEM ESCAPE MORE QUICKLY.

You've probably seen the reaction that happens when you add Mentos candy to a bottle of diet soda. The resulting eruption can be powerful enough to be dangerous and is the source of many online videos! Although many people are familiar with this reaction, few of them understand the science behind why it takes place. Mentos plus soda is not actually a chemical reaction but rather a physical one called nucleation. In this activity, we will explore nucleation in soda at a smaller scale by adding some unusual ingredients to our soda!

PROJECT TIME

20 minutes

KEY CONCEPTS

Chemistry
Reactions
Supersaturation
Nucleation

BACKGROUND

Carbonated drinks, such as soda, are in a state of supersaturation, meaning soda is completely saturated with carbon dioxide (CO_2). Once any solution is supersaturated it generally can't hold any more of the saturating substance. If you add sugar continuously to a glass of water, for example, eventually you'll reach a point when the sugar just sinks to the bottom of the glass instead of dissolving into the water. If you heat the solution of sugar and water, however, the water will be able to accept more of the sugar than it could when the water was cool or at room temperature. Once the heated water has cooled to room temperature it will be supersaturated with sugar—more sugar will have been dissolved in the water than would normally be possible at room temperature.

Carbon dioxide is added to water to make soda in a similar manner. The water has been supersaturated with CO_2 and then bottled and sealed to keep the carbon dioxide dissolved in the soda. The CO_2 is always trying to escape from the soda, and once the soda bottle is open you see so many small bubbles forming, coming out of the solution.

MATERIALS

- Two cans of cold soda
- 1 tablespoon of sugar
- 1 tablespoon of salt
- 1 tablespoon (15 ml) of oil
- Four cups
- Measuring cup (capable of measuring 1/4 cup [60 ml])
- Teaspoon

PREPARATION

- Measure 1/4 cup (60 ml) of soda into each cup.

PROCEDURE

- Slowly add 1 tablespoon of sugar to the first cup. *What happens to the soda when you add sugar?* Notice the reaction and what you hear, see, and even smell!

- Move on to the next cup of soda. Slowly add 1 tablespoon of salt. *What happens to the soda when you add the salt?* Notice the reaction and what you hear, see, and smell.

- Move on to the next cup and slowly add 1 tablespoon (60 ml) of olive oil. *What happens to the soda when you add the oil?* Notice the reaction and what you hear, see, and smell.

- Taste the fourth cup of soda (with nothing added). This is your control soda.

- Use a teaspoon to taste a very small amount of the soda to which you added sugar. *What do you notice about the taste of the control soda compared with the sugar-added one? Is one more bubbly tasting than the other?*

- If you like, compare the taste of your control soda and sugar-added soda with the salt- and the oil-added sodas. (Taste a very small amount of the test sodas!) *What do you notice about the taste of the control soda compared with the salt- and oil-added sodas? Is one more bubbly tasting than the other? How do these compare with the sugar-added soda?*

EXTRA

Try adding small amounts of other edible kitchen ingredients to your soda such as flour or baking soda. Observe the reactions!

OBSERVATIONS AND RESULTS

In this activity, you added different kitchen compounds to soda and observed the reactions. You should have noticed when you added salt and sugar the soda fizzed, and lots of bubbles rose to the surface of the drink. You should also have observed the sight and sound of the gas leaving as well as fewer bubbles in the soda when you tasted it. Adding the oil, however, had little effect on the bubbles in the soda. The reason for this has to do with how the CO_2 gets into soda and how it behaves once it's there.

The soda is supersaturated with carbon dioxide that is just waiting to escape. Adding sugar and salt gives the CO_2 gas the opportunity to leave the soda. Under certain conditions, such as those in this activity, supersaturated solutions will give up what has been dissolved into them at a far quicker rate than they would if left alone. When you added sugar or salt to soda, the CO_2 in each cup latched onto the tiny bumps on the sugar or salt grains. Those tiny bumps, called nucleation sites, give the CO_2 something to hold onto in the soda as it forms bubbles and escapes. The oil molecules, in contrast, have fewer rough spots than the grains of salt and sugar—and thus fewer nucleation sites. As a result, CO_2 escaped the soda more slowly when you added oil to it.

CLEANUP

Wash and dry the cups and measuring cups you used and put them back where you found them. Recycle the empty soda cans.

Freeze Your Fruit with Science

WHAT'S COOLER THAN COLD? MAKE A SUPERCOOL LIQUID TO CREATE INSTANT ICE CRYSTALS.

Pop science quiz: What happens to water when it reaches 32°F (0°C)? Answer: It freezes! But does water always freeze when it reaches this temperature? Believe it or not, water can sometimes be cooled to temperatures below its freezing point and still remain liquid. In this state, the water is supercool. How can this happen? In this activity, you will create your own supercool water and initiate its transition from liquid to solid—all while making a tasty snack!

PROJECT TIME

1 hour, plus 2 hours of freezing time

KEY CONCEPTS

Chemistry
Crystallization
Freezing
Molecules

BACKGROUND

When water is warm or even room temperature, its molecules are moving around, bumping into one another. The warmer the water, the higher the energy of its molecules and the more they collide with one another. In contrast, as water cools, its molecules move more slowly until they eventually almost stop moving altogether. In a frozen state, water molecules are locked together in a crystalline array. These crystals are thought to form around impurities in the water such as dust and minerals. Without the presence of these impurities, however, the water can be supercooled past its freezing point.

In this activity, you will create a bath using salt and ice. Adding the salt results in a bath with a temperature below water's freezing point, a phenomenon known as freezing point depression. You will use this bath to supercool the pure water it surrounds. Then you will perform some supercool tests on this water!

MATERIALS

- Ice
- Fresh fruit, cut into large chunks (at least three pieces)
- Wooden skewers (at least three)
- Two tall, clear, clean plastic cups
- Two large metal or glass bowls
- Two kitchen thermometers (If you only have one, you can switch it between your two cups.)
- Freezer
- Distilled water
- Clock or timer
- 4 to 5 tablespoons of salt
- Cardboard
- Scissors (and an adult's help if needed)

PREPARATION

- Put one piece of fruit on each skewer.
- Place the skewers in the freezer for two hours.
- Carefully cut two circles out of the cardboard, large enough to act as lids for the plastic cups.

PROCEDURE

- Fill each small cup one-third full of filtered water.
- Place one cup in the center of each large metal bowl.
- Cover the plastic cups with your cardboard lids.
- Surround each cup with ice. Make sure the ice is well packed around the cups and comes up higher than the height of the water in the cups. Don't get any ice inside the cups.
- Sprinkle at least 2 tablespoons of salt over the ice. Don't get any salt inside the cups!
- Remove the cardboard lids from the cups.
- Monitor the temperature of the water in your cups using your thermometer(s). If you only have one thermometer, keep it in one cup until the water in that cup cools to below 30°F (-1°C). At that point, you can remove the thermometer and check the temperature in the other cup.
- Once the water has reached a temperature of less than 30°F (-1°C) your water is supercooled! This should take approximately 45 minutes.
- Carefully remove the thermometer and set it aside.
- Remove the frozen fruit skewers from the freezer. *What do you notice about the surface of your fruit? Does it have ice on it?*
- Gently dip a piece of fruit (still on the skewer) into the first cup of supercooled water. Watch what happens to the fruit when it touches the water. *What do you notice about the water surrounding the fruit? What about the fruit itself?*

- Carefully remove the fruit from the water. Look at the fruit. *What do you notice about the fruit's surface?*
- If there is any water left in the first cup, test the temperature of the remaining water. Wait for it to become supercool again, then repeat this experiment with your remaining fruit skewers!
- For the second cup, take a fresh piece of ice (without any salt on it) and carefully drop it into your cup. *What happens to the water in the cup when the ice reaches it? How does this compare with what happened to the fruit?*

OBSERVATIONS AND RESULTS

In this activity, you made water really cold—in fact, you made it supercool! To understand what this means, imagine the molecules that make up the water in your cups. When water is warm or room temperature, those molecules move around, bouncing off one another and the sides of the cups.

When you remove the heat energy from the water in the cups, however, those molecules slow down and eventually nearly stop moving. When they practically stop moving, the molecules form crystals, like those you see creating frost on your windows or drifting from the sky as snowflakes. Crystals don't just form on their own. Before you have a crystal, you need a seed, something for the water molecules to hold onto as they arrange themselves. The water you used in your cups was distilled water and therefore generally free of contaminants such as dust and microbes. As a result, there wasn't anything in the water for the molecules to crystallize around. Therefore, instead of crystalizing when it reached its freezing point, the water remained liquid.

This changed when you added your fruit and your ice cube to the water! The fruit and ice acted as the seed in your supercooled water and gave the water molecules something to crystalize around. In the case of the fruit, the ice crystals you noticed on the surface of the fruit acted as the seed. And in the second cup the ice itself was the seed!

CLEANUP

Wash the cups and bowls and return other materials to the places where you found them.

Make Boba for Bubble Tea

LEARN HOW TO MAKE TASTY BOBA SPHERES OUT OF THREE EASY INGREDIENTS IN THIS TEA-RIFFIC EXPERIMENT.

Have you ever seen "bubble tea" and wondered what the boba spheres in this drink are—and how they are made? Bubble tea or "boba tea" is a sweetened drink made of flavored tea, milk, and bubbles. The translucent, squishy bubbles called boba are very easy to make. You only need three ingredients: tapioca flour, water, and brown sugar. The secret lies in one detail: the temperature of the water. Curious? Try it out and make a bubble beverage from scratch!

PROJECT TIME

1 hour

KEY CONCEPTS

Chemistry
Food Science
Solution
Temperature
Starch

BACKGROUND

The bubbles in bubble tea are made from tapioca flour, which is a starch. Unlike wheat flour, which contains starches, protein, and fiber, tapioca flour contains only starch. And the secret to making bubbles lies in the way starch particles interact with water.

Starch particles are created when a large number of glucose (a form of sugar) units join together. When these particles are mixed with cold water they disperse and float around in the water. This type of mixture is called a suspension, and the suspension of starch in cold water is often referred to as goo or Oobleck. Note that the starch particles do not change when mixed with cold water. When you leave the goo out the water will eventually evaporate, and you will have your starch particles again.

The story changes when you add heat. Starch particles swell and break apart when mixed with hot water. The smaller pieces then create new connections and form a network that can hold water. This process is called starch gelatinization. When this solution cools, it becomes more gel-like. With time it will lose water and become stiffer. But no matter how long you wait, it will not turn into starch particles again. The addition of heat changed the particles.

MATERIALS

- Stovetop
- Pot
- Water
- Measuring cup
- Measuring spoons
- Brown sugar
- Slotted spoon
- Large bowl
- Tapioca flour (also called tapioca starch)
- Small spoon
- Two small bowls or cups
- Cutting board
- Butter knife
- Adult helper
- Glass of cold non-caffeinated tea with milk (optional)
- Other types of flour, such as corn starch, potato starch, or wheat flour (optional)

PREPARATION

- Ask an adult for help any time you need to handle the stove or hot water.
- Heat 3 cups (0.7 l) of water on the stove until the water boils.
- Add 1 cup of brown sugar and stir until the sugar dissolves and forms a syrup. Pour the syrup into a large bowl and set aside to cool.
- Boba, also called tea bubbles or tapioca pearls, are tapioca flour balls cooked in a sugary syrup. You will make two batches: one using cold or room temperature water and another made with boiling hot water. *Do you think using cool or hot water will impact the result? If so, how?*
- Put a small amount of water in a pan on the stove and allow it to heat to a boil as you prepare the tapioca flour.
- Have room temperature or cold water on hand as well.

PROCEDURE

- While the water is heating up on the stove, measure 6 teaspoons of tapioca flour into a small bowl. Add 6 teaspoons of tapioca flour into a second small bowl.
- Start with one bowl with tapioca flour. Have a small spoon ready so you are prepared to start mixing. Pour 2 teaspoons (10 ml) of room temperature or cold water on the tapioca flour and mix the flour with the water right away. Mix it well and set aside.
- Take the second bowl with tapioca flour. Once the water on the stove is boiling ask an adult to measure 2 teaspoons (10 ml) of boiling water and pour it on the tapioca flour. With your small spoon, start mixing the flour with the hot water as soon as it is poured in. Mix well.

- Look at the two batches of dough. *How are they similar? How are they different?*

- One of your doughs is likely clumped together whereas the other one has not. *Why do you think this happens? Which one is clumped—the hot water or cool water one?*

- Set aside the dough that is not clumping.

- Knead the clumping dough with your hands to make a ball. The dough should feel like playdough. Add a tiny amount of hot water if the dough is too dry or a little flour if it is too sticky.

- While you are kneading the dough, ask an adult to heat up 2 cups (473 ml) of the sugar-and-water syrup solution you made earlier in a pot on the stove. Leave 1 cup (237 ml) in a cool place—you will use it later.

- While the syrup heats, transfer the dough to a cutting board, and use your hands to roll it into cylinders with the thickness of a pencil (about 0.04 inch [5 mm] thick). Cut each long cylinder into short pieces that are about as long as they are wide. Roll each little piece into a ball. These are your homemade tapioca boba balls!

- Once the syrup is boiling, have an adult add the balls to the boiling syrup (carefully so as not to splash the hot liquid) and cook them. *Do the balls initially sink or float? Does that change as the cooking process takes place? Why would that happen?*

- Check the progress of the cooking balls every five minutes to see if your bubbles are soft and gooey. It often takes about 20 minutes for the tapioca balls to cook (sometimes smaller balls cook faster and larger ones take longer). The balls will become more translucent, and bubbles will appear in the balls as they cook. Carefully check one or two balls for doneness.

- Once you feel the texture is just right, let them cook just a little bit longer.

- Have an adult scoop the boba out of the boiling syrup with a slotted spoon and place them into the leftover cold syrup to cool.
- Let the boba cool and then have a bite!

EXTRA

Make a cup of non-caffeinated tea, let it cool, and add milk and some of the brown sugar syrup if desired. Add boba and enjoy your homemade cup of boba tea!

EXTRA

Try making boba with the dough that did not clump. *What happens? How does it behave differently from the dough made with the hot water?*

EXTRA

Leave the cup of your first dough (the one made with cold water) out for a day or two, stirring occasionally. *How does it change? Why would this happen? Would the same happen with the dough made with boiling water if that dough was left out for several days?* Give it a try.

EXTRA

The bubbles (tapioca pearls) get harder when they cool and when they are left out. Explore what happens when you reheat them.

SCIENCE FAIR IDEA

Substitute the tapioca flour with another flour, such as corn starch, potato starch, or wheat flour. *Can you predict which flours will give similar bubbles—and which ones will not?*

OBSERVATIONS AND RESULTS

Did your solution made with hot water create dough balls that could be rolled and cooked into tapioca pearls or boba bubbles? When mixed with boiling hot water, starch particles break into smaller pieces that partially dissolve in the water. The pieces make new connections, and as the starch-water mixture cools even more connections are formed. As long as there is not too much water, this mixture can hold its structure.

On the other hand, when mixed with cold water, tapioca flour starch particles spread out and float around. They do not create new connections that can keep dough together.

When you cook the dough, more changes occur in the starch particles. The tiny gas bubbles you see appearing in the pearls indicate this change. The pearls get their typical chewy, gel-like and translucent appearance.

If you tried letting this mixture of starch particles and cold water sit for a couple of days, stirring it occasionally, you might have noticed you end up with pure starch flour again. The water evaporates and you are left with unaltered starch particles. And, if you tried letting the tapioca dough created with hot water sit for a couple of days, you might have noticed it dries out but does not become starch flour again. The starch particles were altered when they came into contact with hot water and will not reform into their original starch composition.

CLEANUP

Wash all the materials and return them to the places where you found them.

Fruits Gone Bad?
Discover Enzymatic Browning

TURNING FRUIT BROWN IN A MATTER OF SECONDS? THIS BIOCHEMISTRY ACTIVITY IS BANANAS!

Have you ever wondered why apple slices turn brown once you cut them, or why a yellow banana gets dark spots over time? Both of these phenomena have the same cause: enzymatic browning triggered by an enzyme called polyphenol oxidase (PPO). In this activity, you will find out how this enzyme works by turning a banana from yellow to brown in just a matter of seconds. Then you will explore how you can keep your apple slices looking fresh!

PROJECT TIME

1 hour

KEY CONCEPTS

Biology
Chemistry
Chemical reactions
Enzymes
Food

BACKGROUND

Tons of fruits and vegetables are produced, processed, and shipped on a daily basis so that we can buy them fresh. Many of these pieces of produce, however, never make it into stores. This is because some fruits and vegetables such as apricots, mushrooms, lettuce, and pears degrade over time because of enzymatic browning. You can see this for yourself if you observe a banana for several days or weeks. Would you buy a brown banana? Enzymatic browning is one of the largest causes of quality loss in fruits and vegetables—even though it does not make the food harmful to eat. So what exactly happens during enzymatic browning?

The process occurs over several steps. The enzyme responsible for the browning is called polyphenol oxidase (or PPO). In the presence of oxygen the PPO enzyme changes substances known as phenolic compounds (through a process of oxidation) into different compounds called quinones. The quinones then react with other compounds to form melanin. Melanin is the same dark brown pigment that colors hair, skin, and the irises of our eyes. It also turns fruit and vegetables brown. This reaction, however, usually does not happen within fresh fruits and vegetables because the PPO and the phenolic compounds are separated in produce plant cells.

The enzymatic browning process is only triggered when PPO, phenolic compounds, and oxygen come in contact with one another. This is exactly what happens when a fruit is cut, falls, or is knocked around too much. When fruit tissue is damaged because of heat, cold, age, or mechanical stress, its cells break open and the phenolic compounds and the enzyme are released and mix with oxygen in the air. As a result, the damaged tissue turns brown almost immediately. In this activity, you will see this browning process for yourself and investigate how this reaction can be avoided. So grab some fruit and get started!

MATERIALS

- Banana (yellow with no brown spots)
- Apple
- Stove
- Pot
- Water
- Timer
- Adult helper
- Cutting board
- Knife
- Lemon juice
- Distilled vinegar

- Milk
- Additional one to two bananas (optional)
- Fridge (optional)
- Tape (optional)
- Other fruits and vegetables to test (optional)

PREPARATION

- Fill a pot with tap water.
- With the help of an adult, place the pot on the stove and heat the water until boiling. Always use caution and adult help when working around very hot water.

PROCEDURE

- Take one of your bananas and look closely at its peel. *What color is it? Do you see any brown spots?*
- Carefully dip the bottom third of the banana into the boiling water for 30 seconds. *What happens to the banana when you submerge it in hot water?*
- After the 30 seconds, remove the banana from the boiling water and observe it for another three minutes. *What do you notice? Does the banana look different after a while? How?*
- When the banana has cooled down, peel the banana. Look at the fruit that was inside the peel. *Did you expect the banana to look like that?*
- With the help of an adult cut two slices from the apple on a cutting board. Place each slice onto its side. *How do they look?*
- Poke one of the apple slices with a fork several times. Then observe both slices for 15 to 20 minutes. *How do the apple slices change over time? Do you notice a difference between the two slices? If yes, can you explain why?*

- Cut five more slices from the apple, and place each slice on its side. Immediately after cutting, sprinkle milk on top of the first slice, distilled vinegar on the second slice, lemon juice on the third slice, and water on the fourth slice. Keep the last slice as is. Then poke each apple slice several times with a fork. *What do you think these liquids will do to the apple?*
- Observe all five apple slices for another 15 to 20 minutes. *How are the apple slices different after 15 to 20 minutes? What did each liquid do to the apple slice? Can you explain your results?*

EXTRA

Instead of heating the banana, try exposing it to cold. Place one banana in the fridge for several days. Take a second banana and cover parts of the banana peel with duct tape. Get creative with the pattern of the tape! Then put that banana in the fridge as well. Check on both bananas every day. *Do both bananas change color? How does the second banana look when you remove the tape after a couple of days? What do you think happened?*

SCIENCE FAIR IDEA

Beside bananas and apples, other fruits can also undergo enzymatic browning. Test different fruits or vegetables to see if they are prone to enzymatic browning. Or try the same fruit but test different kinds of that fruit. *How do different kinds of apples compare?*

OBSERVATIONS AND RESULTS

Were you able to change the color of your banana? Most likely, yes! You probably didn't observe a big difference in the banana right after putting it into the boiled water, but within the next 30 seconds and after taking it out of the water it should have turned pretty dark. You should have noticed that the color change only happened where the banana was submerged in the hot water. This is because the boiling water caused heat stress to the cells in the outer layers of the banana peel and destroyed them. As the cells broke open, they released PPO and phenolic compounds, which then reacted with the oxygen of the air to form melanin. Only the peel should have been affected by enzymatic browning as the inner part of the banana was protected by the peel.

If you put a banana in the fridge, the whole banana should have turned brown. As the banana is a tropical fruit, it is evolved for warm temperatures, which is why the banana cells get damaged in the cold. If you taped parts of the banana, however, you should have noticed that underneath the tape the banana kept its yellow color. This is because the tape sealed the banana from the oxygen, which is necessary for the enzymatic browning reaction to happen.

When you cut an apple, its tissue is damaged, and its cells are broken due to mechanical stress. This again triggers enzymatic browning, which you should have observed on the apple slices. When poking the apple slices with a fork, you damaged even more cells and released more enzyme and phenolic compounds, which is why this apple slice should have turned noticeably darker. The PPO content inside a fruit or vegetable determines the degree of its enzymatic browning. This is why some fruits or vegetables, even different types of apples that contain more of these compounds, become darker than others.

When you sprinkled, milk, lemon juice, vinegar, and water over your apple slices you should have noticed that acidic solutions such as vinegar and lemon juice prevented enzymatic browning. This is because PPO doesn't work well in acidic environments, which means that the enzyme stops working or slows down considerably. So next time you eat an apple and don't want it to get brown you know what to do!

CLEANUP

If you would like to and if you used clean implements, you can eat the experimental fruit. You can compost uneaten fruit.

Make Your Own Fizzy Lemonade

SODA ... POP! LEARN HOW TO MAKE YOUR OWN CARBONATION THANKS TO A LITTLE KITCHEN CHEMISTRY.

Did you know there are thousands of different types of soda around the world? Do you think you would like cheese-flavored soda? What about octopus-flavored soda? Although flavors might differ from country to country, one thing all sodas have in common is the bubbles! Soda isn't soda without that fizz—but have you ever wondered how they create those bubbles? In this activity, you will make your own bubbly drink while exploring the reactions that create that famous fizz.

PROJECT TIME

15 minutes

KEY CONCEPTS

Chemistry
Acids
Bases
Chemical reactions

BACKGROUND

Acids and bases are all around us; in our dishwashing liquid, our medicines—even our foods! They're extremely useful in part because they react so strongly to each other. We can use these reactions to help us clean, ease a sick stomach, or make food taste more interesting.

A base is a compound that can donate negatively charged hydroxide ions. When you add a base to water the basic compound will break apart, and the addition of its hydroxide ions makes the solution more basic. Bases are found in many household cleaning supplies as well as in medicine to help neutralize stomach acid for people who suffer from heartburn.

An acid, in contrast, is a compound that can donate a positively charged hydrogen ion (or proton). When you add an acid to water it will come apart, making the solution more acidic with the addition of its hydrogen ions. Although some acids can be dangerous, we also need them to survive. For instance, as we chew, the acid in saliva helps break down food for digestion!

When you combine an acid and a base you initiate an acid-base reaction. When there are an equal number of hydrogen and hydroxide ions present, the acid and base will neutralize each other, forming a salt and water. In this activity, you will explore the reaction that takes place when you combine an acid with a basic carbonate.

MATERIALS

- Cold water
- Two lemons
- About 1 teaspoon of sugar (more or less to taste)
- 1 teaspoon of baking soda
- Plastic or glass cup
- Stirring spoon
- Lemon juicer/press (recommended)
- Knife (for slicing lemons)
- Adult helper

PREPARATION

- Have your adult helper cut both lemons in half.

PROCEDURE

- Use the lemon juicer to squeeze all of the juice from each lemon into your glass. Taste a few drops of the juice. *How would you describe the taste?*
- Add an equal amount of cold water to the lemon juice in your glass. Taste the mixture again. *Does it taste different than just the lemon juice? In what way?*
- Carefully add 1 teaspoon of baking soda. Use your spoon to stir the mixture. *What happens when you add baking soda to the lemon juice? What do you see and hear happening in the glass?*
- Use your spoon to stir 1 teaspoon of sugar into the mixture. Add ice if you want it cold!
- Taste your concoction! *What do you notice about the taste? How does it differ from the lemon juice alone?*

EXTRA

Allow your mixture to sit for an hour, then taste it again. *How has the taste changed over the course of the hour? Why do you think this change occurred?*

OBSERVATIONS AND RESULTS

In this activity, you should have observed a fizzing or bubbling when you added the baking soda to your lemon juice mixture. In addition, when you tasted your final product, you should have also been able to feel the bubbles in your mouth—which were the product of an acid-base reaction. Can you guess which of the ingredients in your mixture was the acid and which was the base?

If you predicted the lemon juice was the acid, you're right! You can recognize acidic foods (such as lemons, which are very acidic) based on taste; acids taste very sour to us. Other acidic foods include vinegar, grapefruit, and limes. Bases, on the other hand, can be more difficult to detect. Basic foods can taste slightly bitter to us—or they might have very little taste at all. In this case, the base in this mixture was the baking soda, which doesn't have much of a taste. But you might have guessed it was the base in your reaction because as soon as you added it, your mixture should have started fizzing!

When the acid of the lemon juice (citric acid) came in contact with the carbonate base (baking soda), a chemical reaction took place, creating carbon dioxide gas (CO_2). As you may know, CO_2 is the same gas that is added to sodas to give them their fizz.

This reaction requires an acid and a base in order to take place. Therefore, when you tasted just the lemon juice or the lemon juice and water mixture you shouldn't have noticed any bubbles. Water is generally neutral (not an acid or a base)—thus, adding it to your lemon juice did not produce the reaction needed to create CO_2 bubbles. It wasn't until you added the baking soda that the reaction took place, and the bubbles were created.

CLEANUP

Wash all the materials and put them back where you found them. The lemons can be composted.

The Scientific Secret of Stretchy Dough

YOU MIGHT KNOW THE PRODUCTS, BUT DO YOU KNOW THE SECRET OF GREAT DOUGH? WITH A LITTLE BIT OF CHEMISTRY—AND SOME KNEADING—YOU CAN FIND OUT WHAT FLOURS MAKE THE BEST DOUGH—AND WHY.

Do you remember the last time you baked cookies, bread, or cake? Did your baked good turn out perfectly? Or was it a bit too flat or perhaps rubbery and tough, or maybe with clumps of dry ingredients? The problem might have been in how you mixed the dough—or with the type of flour you used. In this science activity, you will knead, stretch, and punch some pretty remarkable doughs and discover what provides structure and elasticity to your baked goods. Next time you prepare dough for bread, pizza, cookies, cake, pie, or any other baked good, you'll know what to do!

PROJECT TIME

45 minutes to 1 hour

KEY CONCEPTS

Chemistry
Food science
Protein
Elasticity

BACKGROUND

Wheat flours mainly consist of carbohydrates and protein, with some fiber. They are classified according to their gluten (or protein) content for a good reason. Getting the right portion of gluten (the protein that naturally occurs in wheat) is essential to getting the right texture in your baked goods. Wonder why? From the moment you bring a liquid ingredient (such as milk or water) in contact with wheat flour, the individual gluten proteins in the flour unravel and hook onto one another, creating strong bonds. With time, an elaborate network of interconnected gluten strings forms. This network holds the dough together, giving it its structure.

Kneading the dough slowly unfolds the entangled network and aligns the long gluten strings in a stretchy, layered web. A pinch of salt helps as well because it neutralizes electrically charged parts of the gluten, allowing them to better slide along one another. The result is an elastic, stretchable dough that traps gas bubbles. Sometimes a dough can be stretched so thin it becomes translucent, making the network of gluten visible with a magnifying glass or microscope. It is the absence of this intricate gluten network that makes gluten-free baking a challenge.

Ready to test and measure your strength against some incredibly stretchy dough? Once you've explored the dough, you'll be ready to bake up a perfect treat!

MATERIALS

- Vital wheat gluten (This is available in well-stocked grocery stores or health food stores.)
- Wheat flour (Bread flour is preferable, but any wheat flour is fine.)
- Gluten-free flour (This could be rice flour, corn flour, a gluten-free baking flour mix, etcetera.)
- Salt
- Measuring cup (1/2 cup)
- Mixing bowl
- Tablespoon measuring spoon
- Spoon
- Water
- Clean work space

PREPARATION

- Choose a work space that is easy to clean and can take some water spills.
- Get all your ingredients out and ready to use.

PROCEDURE

- Combine a pinch of salt with 1/2 cup of vital wheat gluten in your mixing bowl. Add 3 tablespoons (45 ml) of water and mix, first with the spoon, then with your hands. Add 1 or 2 more tablespoons (15 to 30 ml) of water, if needed, until the flour sticks together and forms a nice soft ball. It should have the consistency of playdough. Place the ball on a clean spot on your work space.
- Clean your mixing bowl and measuring utensils then repeat the previous step with 1/2 cup of wheat flour and then again with 1/2 cup of gluten-free flour. *How do the different flours feel? Does one stick together better than the other?*
- Knead your gluten dough for three minutes. To knead, start by flattening the ball of dough a little. Then fold the dough over itself and flatten as you end the fold. Give the dough a quarter turn and repeat the folding, flattening, and turning.
- Repeat the previous step with the wheat flour dough and the gluten-free dough. *Are some doughs easier to knead than others?* You might notice that some doughs fall apart as you try to knead them. If so, just take note and skip kneading that dough.
- Let your dough balls rest for one half hour.
- While you wait, look at the nutritional content label of the flours printed on the packages. *Which one has more carbohydrates per one-quarter cup serving, and which one has more protein?*

- In a moment you will test how elastic the doughs are and how easily they can be stretched. Elasticity measures how well a material recovers its original form after a deformation. *Which dough do you expect to be elastic, meaning it bounces back after you punch it? Which dough do you expect to be starchiest? Do you expect you will be able to stretch any of the doughs paper-thin?*

- Now that you have given the gluten network in the doughs some time to develop, you can put them to the test. Lightly punch your balls of dough—all three with the same force—to evaluate their elasticity. *Do you see signs of elasticity in any of your doughs? Can you rank them from most elastic to least, or nonelastic?*

- A second characteristic is stretchiness. A dough that stretches well can trap gas bubbles, providing well-risen, fluffy baked goods. Take a ball in two hands and stretch it out between your hands. *Does it stretch easily, or does it break instantly? Do you need to apply force to get it to stretch out or does it stretch readily?* Do this with all three doughs.

- Some pastries require a paper-thin layer of dough. *How thin can you stretch out or roll out your doughs? Can you make any of them so thin that you can almost look through them?*

- *Looking at your test results, what type of baked good would each dough be good for: cake, cookies, bread, etcetera? Why do you think this is the case?*

SCIENCE FAIR IDEA

What would happen if you let the doughs rest for a longer period of time? Would the elasticity or stretchiness increase? Place your doughs in a container or plastic bag and let them rest for a few hours or overnight. This allows the flours to fully absorb the water and the gluten networks to fully develop. Perform your tests again. *Do you notice considerable changes?*

EXTRA

Place each dough ball in its own bowl, cover each with water, and let them soak awhile. Play with each ball; pinch and knead it a little and see what happens. Carbohydrates will wash out whereas the gluten network will create an elastic ball. *After washing away all the carbohydrates, what do you think will be left in each type of dough?* Try it out and see if your prediction was correct.

SCIENCE FAIR IDEA

Gluten has several functions in dough. It binds ingredients and provides structure to the dough. It creates elastic doughs that do not need a mold to keep their form. It also helps retain moisture and prolongs the shelf life of the baked goods. Gluten-free dough mixes use xanthan gum, guar gum, and/or ground seeds to take over these tasks. *Can you bake a gluten-free bead and a wheat bread and compare their performance against these parameters?* You can also bake two wheat breads, one with cake flour (low in gluten) and another with bread flour (high in gluten) and compare their performance against these parameters.

OBSERVATIONS AND RESULTS

Was the gluten dough elastic and stretchable? Did the gluten-free dough fall apart, showing neither elasticity nor stretchiness? This is expected; it is the gluten network that holds dough together and gives it elasticity and the ability to stretch.

Combine gluten and water, and a network of long, unorganized, knotted gluten strings will form. Kneading aligns these strings, creating a dough you might be able to stretch so thin you can almost see through it. The more gluten, the more elastic, stretchy, and strong the dough will be. Mixing gluten and water results in a dough that almost feels like rubber. Wheat flour contains 6 to 12 percent gluten, enough to provide a gluten network that holds the carbohydrates together. This dough is elastic and stretchy, but not as strong and tough as the gluten dough. A gluten-free dough, on the other hand, is crumbly; it falls apart easily. Bakers add ingredients such as xanthan gum, guar gum, and/or ground seeds to keep the baked goods together—but making a gluten-free version of some fine pastries, fluffy croissants, and delicate wheat breads can be challenging!

CLEANUP

Wash your materials and put them back where you found them.

Sweet and Sour Science You Can Taste!

MAKE SOME SCIENCE THAT FIZZES AND POPS—IN YOUR MOUTH!

Did you know that the juices in your stomach are nearly as acidic as lemon juice? Fortunately, your stomach has special cells that act as a barrier to the acid, preventing it from breaking down your stomach tissue. These cells produce a basic mucus that neutralizes the acid in your stomach. It turns out that your stomach is a pretty sophisticated chemistry laboratory!

In this activity, you'll explore a delicious acid-base reaction, this time using your mouth as the chemistry lab!

PROJECT TIME

20 minutes

KEY CONCEPTS

Chemistry
Acids
Bases
Ions
Reactions

BACKGROUND

We use acids and bases every day—they're present in our foods, our cosmetics, and our cleaning supplies. We're so used to them that it's easy to forget how interesting they are and how much our daily activities depend on the reactions they generate.

An acid is a compound that is capable of donating a positively charged hydrogen ion (or proton). If you add an acid to water, it breaks apart and makes the solution more acidic by adding hydrogen ions. Acids come in many different strengths and are essential to our daily lives. We couldn't digest our food without the acid in our stomachs!

Bases are also extremely important in our lives. A base is a compound capable of donating negatively charged hydroxide ions. If you add a base to water, it breaks apart and makes the solution more basic by adding hydroxide ions.

When acids and bases are combined, an acid-base reaction occurs. If there are an equal number of hydrogen and hydroxide ions present, the acid and base will neutralize each other, forming a salt and water. In this activity, you will explore the reaction that takes place when you combine an acid with a basic carbonate. The product of this reaction is a fun and tasty surprise!

MATERIALS

- Three small, sealable plastic sandwich bags
- 6 tablespoons confectioners' sugar
- 9 tablespoons gelatin crystals (the flavored kind works best)
- 2 teaspoons baking soda
- 2 teaspoons citric acid (available in the spice/baking section)
- Permanent marker
- Measuring spoon (teaspoon and tablespoon)
- Regular spoon
- Glass of drinking water

PREPARATION

- Use your marker to label your bags. Label bag one: "Acid + Soda"; bag two: "Acid Only"; and bag three: "Soda Only."

PROCEDURE

- Carefully measure and add 2 tablespoons of confectioners' sugar to each bag.
- Carefully measure and add 3 tablespoons of gelatin crystals to each bag.
- Add 1 teaspoon of citric acid to the bag labeled "Acid + Soda." Add another teaspoon of citric acid to the bag labeled "Acid Only."
- Add 1 teaspoon of baking soda to the bag labeled "Acid + Soda." Add another teaspoon of baking soda to the bag labeled "Soda Only."
- Seal each bag, then shake them to mix the ingredients together. *Does anything happen to the ingredients when you mix them together? Is there any kind of reaction that you can observe?*
- Once the ingredients are well mixed open the bag labeled "Acid Only." Use your spoon to take a small scoop of the bag contents and put them in your mouth. Hold the ingredients on your tongue for a moment before swallowing them. *What does it taste like? Can you feel anything happening in your mouth when you taste them?*
- Take a drink of water and rinse your mouth thoroughly.
- Open the bag labeled "Acid + Soda." Use your spoon to take a small scoop of the bag contents and put them in your mouth. Hold the ingredients on your tongue for a moment before swallowing them. *What does it taste like? Do you notice anything different about this taste test, compared to the "Acid Only" bag? What is different?*
- Take a drink of water and rinse your mouth thoroughly.

- Open the bag labeled "Soda Only." Use your spoon to take a small scoop of the bag contents and put them in your mouth. Hold the ingredients on your tongue for a moment before swallowing them. *What does it taste like? Which taste test is this most similar to, the first one, or the second one?*

EXTRA

Try changing the proportion of ingredients, adding 1/2 a teaspoon more acid or soda, and see how it changes the reaction.

OBSERVATIONS AND RESULTS

In this activity, your mouth was a mini-chemistry lab! When you tasted the "Acid + Soda" bag contents, you should have felt a fizzing or popping sensation in your mouth. When the acid (citric acid) and carbonate base (baking soda) mixed with your saliva, a chemical reaction took place that created carbon dioxide gas—which you felt as tiny bubbles in your mouth. The dry ingredients also react with each other, but it's a much slower reaction. When you add them to your mouth, the saliva helps the acid and base dissolve, increasing the chances that a bicarbonate ion will come in contact with an acidic proton. The reaction, therefore, takes place much more quickly, and you can feel the gas bubbles produced!

An acid-base reaction like this one requires two main ingredients—can you guess what they are? An acid and a base! So when you tasted the contents of the "Acid Only" or the "Base Only" bag you shouldn't have felt any chemical reaction occur. In both cases you were missing a critical ingredient. With the "Acid Only" bag, you had citric acid but no baking soda, therefore the acid didn't have a base to react with. In the case of the "Base Only" bag, the baking soda did not have an acid to react with.

You might have also noticed that each bag tasted slightly different. Baking soda is a salt; it is also called sodium bicarbonate. You might have noticed that the "Soda Only" bag tasted slightly saltier than the other two bags. Acids such as citric acid, in contrast, often taste sour to us (think about citrus fruits with high citric acid content, such as lemons, limes, and grapefruit). You might, therefore, have noticed that the "Acid Only" bag tasted more sour than the other two bags.

CLEANUP

All ingredients can be thrown away. Clean all materials and return them to the places where you found them.

Soft-Boiled Science
Eggs-cellently Cooked Eggs

LEARN THE SECRETS TO COOKING THE PERFECT SOFT-BOILED EGG FOR YOUR MORNING BREAKFAST!

Have you ever been in such a rush in the morning that you barely had time for breakfast? Eggs can be a good breakfast choice because they can be cooked quickly and in many different ways. Eggs have been eaten for thousands of years, all over the world. Hard-boiled eggs are commonly used for dying Easter eggs, but a soft-boiled egg can make a yummy breakfast or snack. How does different exposure to heat at different times change the way an egg cooks? In this activity, you'll determine the best recipe for producing consistent, soft-boiled eggs that will get your day off to a great start!

PROJECT TIME

30 minutes, plus an hour of warming time

KEY CONCEPTS

Food science
Proteins
Heat
Eggs

BACKGROUND

The typical egg packs a big punch in a small package. One large egg has about 75 calories, many essential nutrients, lots of high-quality protein, various vitamins, multiple minerals, choline, folate, and riboflavin. Eggs can help you maintain muscle strength as well as promote a healthy brain and eye function. The yolk contains the fat of the egg, most of the vitamins and minerals, and about half of the protein. The albumen (egg white) is mostly water (about 90 percent) and protein (about 10 percent).

There are several methods for preparing eggs. They can be scrambled, poached, fried, pickled, hard-boiled, and soft-boiled. In a raw egg, the proteins in the egg are folded and curled up tight. But when you cook an egg, the heat causes its proteins to uncurl so that they interact with one another, forming a network of connected proteins. In a soft-boiled egg, the white is firm, but the yolk is between runny and solid—in other words, the yolk should be viscous, or thickened and sticky.

MATERIALS

- Three raw eggs
- Pot with lid
- Ice cubes
- Water
- Large bowl
- Plates
- Stove top (adult supervision is recommended while using the stove and handling any hot items)
- Slotted spoon
- Timer

PREPARATION

- If the eggs are being stored in the refrigerator, take them out and let them warm to room temperature. This may take about an hour.

- Remember to always wash your hands with soap and warm water after handling uncooked eggs because they can carry salmonella. For this same reason, it is not recommended that you eat any uncooked eggs you prepare in this activity.

- Gently place an egg in a pot and add water. Fill the pot so that the egg is covered by about 1 inch (2.5 cm) of water.
- Put several ice cubes in a large bowl and fill it with enough water to cover an egg. This will be your ice water bath. If many of the ice cubes melt during the activity, add new ones to the bowl.

PROCEDURE

- Place the pot of water with the egg in it on the stove top, put the lid on the pot, and bring the water to a boil. (Please have adult supervision when operating the stove and handling hot items.)
- Once the water is vigorously boiling, let the egg cook for five minutes. Keep the lid on the pot during this time.
- After boiling for five minutes, carefully remove the egg using the slotted spoon and place it into the ice water bath.
- Let the egg sit in the bath for one minute, then remove the egg, peel it, and place it on a plate.
- Observe the egg. *Is the white firm or watery? How thick is the solid white? Is the yolk slimy, viscous, or hard? Overall, does it seem like the egg is soft-boiled?*
- Bring the water in the pot back up to a vigorous boil and use the slotted spoon to carefully place a new raw egg into the boiling water. Let the egg boil for five minutes (with the lid on the pot).
- After five minutes, carefully remove the egg and place it into the ice water bath. Let the egg sit there for one minute, then remove it, peel it, and place it on a plate.
- Observe the egg. *Is the white firm or watery? How thick is the solid white? Is the yolk slimy, viscous, or hard? Overall, does it seem like the egg is soft-boiled?*

- Bring the water in the pot back up to a vigorous boil and carefully place a new raw egg into the boiling water. Once the egg is submerged, turn off the stove and move the pot to a cool burner. Let the egg steep in the just-boiled water for five minutes. Leave the lid off the pot while the egg steeps.
- After five minutes, carefully remove the egg and place it into the ice water bath. Let the egg sit for one minute, then remove it, peel it, and place it on a plate.
- Observe the egg. *Is the white firm or watery? How thick is the solid white? Is the yolk slimy, viscous, or hard? Overall, does it seem like the egg is soft-boiled?*
- *Which cooking method seemed to lead to the best soft-boiled egg: bringing the egg and water up to a boil together, just cooking the egg in already boiling water, or steeping the egg in just-boiled water? If they showed similar results, which method seemed to use less energy?*

EXTRA

Eggs come in different sizes. You could try three different sizes of eggs with the method that worked best for you in this activity. *Does the size of the egg affect how well the best soft-boiling recipe works?*

SCIENCE FAIR IDEA

You could try this activity again but increase or decrease the amount of time that the egg is in hot water. *Can you perfect the soft-boiling recipe?*

OBSERVATIONS AND RESULTS

Was the egg that was brought to a boil along with the water overcooked, being more similar to a hard-boiled egg than a soft-boiled one? Were the other eggs much closer to being soft-boiled?

When the egg and water were brought up to a boil together, the egg was probably fairly hard-boiled, with a completely firm, thick white and a hard yolk (although it may have had a slightly less cooked, more orange area in the very center). The egg that was steeped in the just-boiled water should have been much more watery, with a much less firm white that was mostly white (but maybe clear in places) and a slimy yolk. Depending on the exact conditions used, however, this egg may have been slightly more cooked and appeared soft-boiled. The recipe that probably resulted in the most soft-boiled-like egg was just cooking the egg in the already boiling water, which cooked the egg more than did steeping it in the just-boiled water, but less than bringing the egg and water up to a boil together. Another common approach to soft-boiling eggs is using simmering, instead of boiling water. What other commonly made foods can you use science to help perfect the recipe?

CLEANUP

Always wash your hands with soap and warm water after handling uncooked eggs because they can carry salmonella. Be sure to also wash objects, such as plates, that came into contact with the uncooked eggs. For this same reason, it is not recommended that you eat any uncooked or partially cooked eggs you prepared in this activity.

THE SCIENTIFIC METHOD

The scientific method helps scientists—and students—gather facts to prove whether an idea is true. Using this method, scientists come up with ideas and then test those ideas by observing facts and drawing conclusions. You can use the scientific method to develop and test your own ideas!

Question: What do you want to learn? What problem needs to be solved? Be as specific as possible.
Research: Learn more about your topic and refine your question.
Hypothesis: Form an educated guess about what you think will answer your question. This allows you to make a prediction you can test.
Experiment: Create a test to learn if your hypothesis is correct. Limit the number of variables, or elements of the experiment that could change.
Analysis: Record your observations about the progress and results of your experiment. Then analyze your data to understand what it means.
Conclusion: Review all your data. Did the results of the experiment match the prediction? If so, your hypothesis was correct. If not, your hypothesis may need to be changed.

GLOSSARY

alter: To change.
concoction: A mixture with various ingredients.
contaminant: Something that makes a substance no longer able to be used.
dilute: To add water to something.
disperse: To spread out.
extract: Remove or take out.
impurity: Something that makes a substance not its pure form.
initiate: To cause to begin.
intermittently: Not continuously or steadily.
intricate: Complicated or detailed.
neutralize: To make a substance equal parts acid and base.
prolong: Extend.
prone: Likely to experience.
translucent: Partially see-through.
viscous: Having a thick, sticky consistency.

ADDITIONAL RESOURCES

Books

Adams, William D. *Chemistry Everywhere!* Chicago, IL: World Book, 2023.

Biberdorf, Kate. *Kate the Chemist: The Awesome Book of Edible Experiments for Kids.* New York, NY: Philomel Books, 2022.

Holiday Science: 10 Fun Chemistry and Food Science Projects. New York, NY: Scientific American Educational Publishing, an imprint of Rosen Publishing, 2023.

Tobler, Elise. *What Are Mixtures?* New York, NY: Gareth Stevens Publishing, 2022.

Websites

Discovery Education
sciencefaircentral.com

Exploratorium
www.exploratorium.edu/explore/activities

Science Buddies
www.sciencebuddies.org/science-fair-projects/project-ideas/list

Science Fun for Everyone!
www.sciencefun.org/?s=science+fair

Videos

Cooking with Bill Nye | NOVA
https://wtvi.pbslearningmedia.org/resource/arct14.sci.nvnyecook/cooking-with-bill-nye-nova/

Fizzy Fun and Exploring Acid-Base Chemistry | Cooking Up Science with Miss America
https://wtvi.pbslearningmedia.org/resource/acid-base-chemistry-video/science-cooking-miss-america/

The Science of Cooking and Baking | Cooking Up Science with Miss America
https://wtvi.pbslearningmedia.org/resource/science-cooking-baking-video/science-cooking-miss-america/

Publisher's note to educators and parents: Our editors have carefully reviewed these websites to ensure that they are suitable for students. Many websites change frequently, however, and we cannot guarantee that a site's future contents will continue to meet our high standards of quality and educational value. Be advised that students should be closely supervised whenever they access the internet.

INDEX